## Math in My World

# Math at the Store

### By William Amato

Children's Press®
A Division of Scholastic Inc.
New York / Toronto / London / Auckland / Sydney
Mexico City / New Delhi / Hong Kong
Danbury, Connecticut

*Thanks to Kyj's Bakery, Brookhaven, PA*

Photo Credits: Cover and all photos by Maura Boruchow
Contributing Editor: Jennifer Silate
Book Design: Laura Stein

Library of Congress Cataloging-in-Publication Data

Amato, William.
Math at the store / by William Amato.
     p. cm. — (Math in my world)
   Includes index.
Summary: Simple text and pictures show how math can be used in buying food at the store.
   ISBN 0-516-23937-6 (lib. bdg.) — ISBN 0-516-23595-8 (pbk.)
   1. Mathematics—Juvenile literature. [1. Mathematics.] I. Title.

 QA40.5 .A52 2002
 510—dc21

                                              2001032341

# Contents

My name is Kate.

Tomorrow is my birthday!

november

| | 4 | 5 | 6 | 7 | 8 | 9 | 10 |
| | 11 | 12 | 13 | 14 | 15 | 16 | 17 |
| | 19 | 20 | 21 | 22 | 23 | 24 | |
| 25 | 26 | 27 | 28 | 29 | 30 | | |

5

Mom and I are going to buy cupcakes.

I will take them to school and share them with my class tomorrow.

Fifteen **students** are in my class.

I will buy one cupcake for each student.

9

I get five
**chocolate** cupcakes.

I also get five
**vanilla** cupcakes.

How many cupcakes
do I have?

I have ten cupcakes.

How many more cupcakes
do I need?

13

I need five more cupcakes.

I will get five more
vanilla cupcakes!

15

Now, we must pay for
the cupcakes.

We take them to
the **cashier**.

The cupcakes cost fifteen **dollars**.

Mom gives the cashier twenty dollars.

How much money do we get back?

We get five dollars back.

I cannot wait to go to school tomorrow!

21

# New Words

cashier  (ka-**shihr**) someone who is in charge of money in a business

chocolate  (**chawk**-liht) a flavoring made from roasted and ground cacao beans

dollars  (**dahl**-uhrz) units of money in Canada or the United States; one dollar is equal to one hundred cents

students  (**stood**-nts) people who study in a school

vanilla  (vuh-**nihl**-uh) a flavoring made from the bean of a plant

# To Find Out More

## Books

*Pigs Go to Market: Fun with Math and Shopping*
by Amy Axelrod
Simon & Schuster Children's Press

*Cats Add Up!*
by Dianne Ochiltree
Scholastic, Inc.

## Web Site

**Cool Math 4 Kids**
http://www.coolmath4kids.com
This Web site has fun games and math problems for kids of all ages.

# Index

About the Author

William Amato is a teacher and writer living in New York City.

Reading Consultants

Kris Flynn, Coordinator, Small School District Literacy, The San Diego County Office of Education

Shelly Forys, Certified Reading Recovery Specialist, W.J. Zahnow Elementary School, Waterloo, IL

Sue McAdams, Former President of the North Texas Reading Council of the IRA, and Early Literacy Consultant, Dallas, TX